Original title:
Dappled Grips Across the Witch Fang

Author: Daisy Dewi
ISBN HARDBACK: 978-1-80562-362-5
ISBN PAPERBACK: 978-1-80563-883-4

The Haunting of the Olden Throne

In a castle draped in twilight's shroud,
Echoes of whispers linger loud.
Shadows dance upon the stone,
Guarding secrets long overgrown.

Ghostly wraiths in tattered gowns,
Flicker softly, casting frowns.
Memories woven in silver light,
Buried deep in endless night.

The throne sits cold, a regal sight,
Once ruled by kings of shining might.
Now it crumbles, the past entwined,
With tales of love and fate maligned.

Through the windows, moonlight spills,
Filling chambers with forgotten thrills.
But every smile holds a tear,
A story lost to ancient years.

If you listen beside the hearth,
You may hear the laughter's worth.
Though time has turned the page so rough,
The olden throne is still enough.

Prints of Shadows on the Forest Floor

Beneath the boughs of whispering trees,
Footprints linger in the breeze.
Each mark a tale of fleeting friends,
Where the wild enchantment never ends.

Mossy carpets, soft and green,
Hiding wonders seldom seen.
Flickering lights of firefly glow,
Guide the weary wayward soul.

Songs of crickets fill the air,
Twinkling stars, a night so rare.
Yet shadows loom, they twist and creep,
In secrets that the forest keeps.

Echoes ring through ancient glade,
Where dreams are born and fears portrayed.
With every rustle, every sigh,
The woods hold whispers that never die.

So tread with care upon this ground,
Where stories lost may yet be found.
For in the heart of nature's lore,
Lie prints of shadows forevermore.

Patterns in the Witching Hour

In shadows deep where secrets creep,
The whispers of the night do speak.
With silver threads the stars align,
In patterns woven, fate's design.

The moonlight dances on the ground,
With every turn, strange shapes abound.
A tapestry of dreams unfolds,
As magic's hand the hour holds.

Ghostly echoes kiss the air,
While owls call from their hidden lairs.
Each flicker of the candle's glow,
Reveals the paths we cannot know.

A flicker here, a shimmer there,
The heart of night begins to bare.
In twilight, secrets old and new,
Awaken spirits, bold and true.

As daylight fades, enchantment stirs,
In every rustle, magic purrs.
Embrace the hour where shadows play,
For patterns bloom in dusk's ballet.

The Enigma of Luminous Claws

In the forest dense, where silence stirs,
Aligned with trees, the mystery whirs.
Bright claws of light through branches shine,
A riddle veiled, a spark divine.

Moonlit shadows dance around,
Each step a heartbeat, deep and profound.
Whispers soft as the nightingale's song,
Guide the wanderers, where they belong.

Glimmering talons pierce the gloom,
Awakening beauty, dispelling doom.
They beckon souls to venture forth,
Into the wonder, they nurture worth.

What secrets lie in glowing hands?
What stories bloom in ancient lands?
Curiosity pulls, and with a sigh,
The truth emerges, nigh on high.

Thus, let the claws of night embrace
The jagged lines of fate's great trace.
For every glow, a tale resides,
In luminous claws, the heart confides.

Reflections in the Celestial Thicket

Among the boughs that touch the sky,
Whispers echo, as wonders fly.
Stars wink softly in the night,
In this thicket, dreams take flight.

Mirrored pools of silver hue,
Reflecting all the soul holds true.
Secrets dance in brimming tides,
Where the heart in silence abides.

The rustle of leaves, a gentle call,
Inviting those who dare to fall.
Into the depths of twilight's spell,
Where stories thrive and shadows dwell.

The cosmos bends in every glance,
As magic weaves a timeless dance.
Celestial whispers, soft and clear,
Guide the lost within their sphere.

So step within this sacred grove,
Where reflections shimmer and dreams erode.
In every sigh, the stars align,
In the celestial thicket, fate we find.

The Spellbound Canopy

Beneath the canopy, a world enchants,
Where wisdom rests in ancient plants.
The rustling leaves sing lines of lore,
Each layer whispering what's in store.

With branches braided, stories weave,
A shelter blessed for those who cleave.
To nature's heart, in silence sway,
The spellbound air holds night at bay.

Glistening droplets fall like tears,
A soothing balm for hidden fears.
The woodland spirits weave their charms,
Embracing all with open arms.

Underneath the shifting light,
Every shadow transforms the night.
A place where dreams and truth collide,
In the spellbound canopy, we bide.

So linger long beneath this shade,
Where echoes call, and fears fade.
For in this realm of twist and sway,
The magic hums, forever play.

The Hall of Shadows and Lost Secrets

In halls where whispers cling so tight,
A tapestry of dark and light.
Forgotten tales in shadows dance,
A haunting pull, a fateful chance.

The echoes of a long-lost song,
Guide the brave who wander wrong.
Illusions bend the path ahead,
Where silence speaks of things unsaid.

The air is thick with ancient lore,
A gateway to the evermore.
With every step, the heart must choose,
To seek the truth or live the ruse.

Amidst the gloom, a flicker glows,
A secret kept where nobody goes.
Each shadow, friend or foe may be,
A dance that masks the mystery.

In this vast expanse of night,
Awaits the dawn, a fragile light.
To unearth what the past conceals,
One must be brave to face what heals.

Enigmatic Nightfall in Haunted Glades

Beneath the boughs of twisted trees,
The night unfolds with secret ease.
Whispers drift like ghostly sighs,
Where flickering starlight softly dies.

The glades are filled with shadowed grace,
A silent waltz in time and space.
With every rustle, magic stirs,
A language found in fleeting blurs.

Comets craft their earthly path,
Igniting dreams beneath their wrath.
Each breath of wind a soft embrace,
Inviting the lost to find their place.

The darkness holds a gentle thrill,
An ancient power, strong and still.
As fireflies weave their glowing thread,
The map of night unfurls ahead.

When dawn's first light begins to break,
The glade awakes, its secrets shake.
But in the twilight's quiet veil,
Adventurers know to heed the trail.

Chants of the Fey in Whispering Leaves

In glades where softest echoes blend,
The Fey weave songs that twist and bend.
With every breath, the leaves will sigh,
In harmony with earth and sky.

Their laughter twirls upon the breeze,
Entwined with secrets of the trees.
A tapestry of glistening dew,
Held captive in a world anew.

Each note a shimmer, light and free,
A calling from the ancient tree.
To join their dance, the heart must yearn,
For magic with a flame that burns.

Beneath the boughs, a shimmer glows,
As nature shares what no one knows.
The whispers shrill, the chants arise,
An echo from the starlit skies.

In every rustle, they invite,
To wander deep into the night.
To leave behind the weight of time,
And taste the sweetness of the rhyme.

The Tangle of Enchantment's Grasp

In webs of dreams, enchantments lie,
A tangle spun where secrets sigh.
With every thread of silk and sound,
A world of wonder can be found.

The whispers call from hidden nooks,
In pages worn of dusty books.
A flicker here can light the way,
Where shadows play and spirits sway.

Beware the lure of golden glow,
For not all paths reveal what's known.
With glimmers bright, temptation glows,
Yet wisdom blooms where caution grows.

For in the heart of darkness lies,
The chains that bind and dreams that rise.
To break the spell, the brave must see,
The nature of their destiny.

With steps of courage, hearts set free,
From every snare, they'll find the key.
In tangled realms, new worlds expand,
Awaking dreams borne from the hand.

Flickering Spirits Beneath the Canopy

In twilight's glow, the shadows dance,
With flickers of light, they weave their trance.
The whispers of leaves, a gentle sigh,
As spirits drift where the lost ones lie.

Mossy stones with secrets keep,
In silent woods where the moonbeams creep.
Their laughter lingers in the air,
A haunting tune of forgotten fare.

Beneath the boughs, where dreams take flight,
They swirl and twirl in the deepening night.
The flickering sparks of starry eyes,
In enchanted glades, where magic lies.

Each breath of wind a tale retold,
Of bravest hearts and treasures bold.
In harmony, the night sings clear,
Of flickering spirits, gathered near.

Glistening Shadows of Silent Sorrow

In the moon's soft glow, shadows tread,
Glistening trails where the fallen fled.
Their echoes, soft as the nightingale,
Carry tales of a sorrowful tale.

Misty veils cloaked in despair,
Hidden grief lingers in the air.
A quiet whisper, a soft lament,
In every breeze, a heart's content.

The weeping willow bows in woe,
As memories ebb and flow.
Among the stones where silence reigns,
Glistening shadows, bearing chains.

But through the dark, hope does gleam,
A fragile thread, a gentle dream.
In sorrow's depth, a light will find,
Glistening shadows, intertwined.

Arcane Whispers Beneath the Oak's Boughs

Beneath the oak, where shadows weave,
Arcane whispers the old trees leave.
In each rustling leaf, a secret lies,
Tales of magic in twilight skies.

The ancient bark, a sage's face,
Guarding riddles of time and space.
With every sigh, the spirits call,
Echoes of wisdom, both grand and small.

Cloaked in shadows, they dance and swirl,
A tapestry where sunlight unfurl.
Their laughter mingles with the breeze,
A symphony played among the leaves.

In this enchanted, sacred room,
The oak bears witness to joy and gloom.
Arcane whispers guide the lost,
To the heart of magic, at any cost.

The Lure of the Bewitching Thicket

In the bewitching thicket, secrets dwell,
Where sweet enchantments weave their spell.
Amongst the blooms of vibrant hue,
The lure of magic calls anew.

Gossamer threads in the evening light,
Guide wandering souls into the night.
With every step, the heartbeats race,
For in the thicket, dreams interlace.

Velvet petals, so soft to touch,
Invite the weary to linger much.
With laughter carried on the breeze,
The thicket beckons with whispered pleas.

Twilight dances, casting shadows long,
In the thicket, where all belong.
Adventure awaits 'neath the verdant cloak,
In the bewitching, unbroken yoke.

Unraveled Threads in the Dark

In shadows deep, where whispers weave,
The threads of fate begin to grieve.
A tapestry of night unfolds,
With secrets held in silence cold.

The moonbeams dance on dreams forlorn,
In tangled paths, hope's light is born.
Yet in the gloom, a flicker bright,
A promise shines to pierce the night.

With every thread that starts to fray,
New roads emerge, come what may.
The heart's desire, a guiding spark,
Unraveled whispers in the dark.

Through corridors of mist and time,
The echo of a distant chime.
Each step is fraught with fate's embrace,
Yet courage finds its rightful place.

So hold the threads, though torn they seem,
For in their weavings lies the dream.
Embrace the night, let shadows sway,
Unraveled threads shall light the way.

Relics of the Starlit Boughs

In twilight's kiss, where starlight gleams,
Ancient whispers share their dreams.
Beneath the boughs, the secrets lie,
As constellations flicker by.

With silver leaves that softly sway,
Each relic tells of yesterday.
The stories etched in time's embrace,
In echoes of a long-lost place.

The moonlight bathes the sacred ground,
In this stillness, magic's found.
With every touch, the past awakes,
A dance of fate that never breaks.

Among the roots, the shadows play,
Where dreams and starlight find their way.
Each whispered tale, a thread of lore,
Relics cherished forevermore.

So linger here, 'neath starlit skies,
Where ancient truths and magic lies.
The boughs will bridge both time and space,
In their embrace, we find our place.

Beneath the Cursed Canopy

In tangled woods where whispers dwell,
A cursed canopy weaves its spell.
With twisted branches, secrets loom,
And shadows dance to the tune of doom.

The air is thick with tales of woe,
In silence deep, the lost ones go.
Each step a choice, a perilous fate,
The cursed trees whisper, "Don't be late."

Yet in the gloom, a flicker's glow,
A guiding light, though soft and low.
Through heartache's path, a courage found,
To break the chains that hold the ground.

Though darkness clings and fears take flight,
The spirit's spark ignites the night.
With every breath, the shadows part,
As bravery blooms within the heart.

Beneath the curses, hope will rise,
Transforming truths that wear disguise.
With every brush of fate's cruel hand,
We'll carve our path and make our stand.

Caresses of the Ethereal Mist

In morning's glow, the mist awakes,
A gentle touch, the silence breaks.
With soft caresses, dreams take flight,
In whispers wrapped in morning light.

The world transformed in dew-kissed grace,
Each leaf's embrace a tender trace.
Through hazy paths, the heart does dance,
In the ethereal mist, a fleeting chance.

With every breath, the spirit sighs,
As sunlight spills from painted skies.
In moments soft, where time stands still,
The heart ignites with fervent will.

So wander through the shrouded days,
In mystery's soft, enchanting ways.
In misty realms where echoes gleam,
Life's tender caresses craft the dream.

Embrace the dawn, the warmth it brings,
The echo of a thousand things.
For in the mist, where shadows blend,
A journey starts, and spirits mend.

Shade Patterns on Enchanted Fangs

In twilight's grasp, where shadows weave,
The fangs of night begin to cleave.
With shades that dance on whispered breath,
They twinkle soft, like dreams of death.

Beneath the moon, they catch the glow,
Reflecting secrets, deep and low.
Each pattern tells a tale untold,
Of ancient magic, fierce and bold.

Among the trees, where silence hums,
The fangs weave stories, yet to come.
Their silver tips in darkness gleam,
A haunting echo of a dream.

In every flicker, a memory bends,
A bond with night that never ends.
The shade they cast, both dark and bright,
A lantern's guide within the night.

So here we stand, by starlit glades,
Where every shadow softly fades,
Entranced by fangs, we find our way,
Through enchanted paths where fancies play.

Whispers of the Forest's Embrace

In velvet dusk, the forest sighs,
With secrets held beneath the skies.
Each whisper wraps around the trees,
A sacred pact with every breeze.

The leaves will croon, in hushed delight,
As shadows gather, cloaked in night.
Soft murmurs brush the ancient bark,
As dreams take flight, igniting spark.

Through twisted roots, the magic flows,
In gentle waves, the twilight glows.
The ferns bow low to hear the song,
Of nature's heart where souls belong.

A dance of light, from stars that twirl,
Each shimmering note begins to whirl.
In every breath, a story shared,
Of love and loss, of hope declared.

So linger here, in twilight's fold,
Where mysteries of the forest hold.
A tender touch from woods so wide,
Whispers of dreams that never hide.

Twilight Shadows and Silvered Teeth

In twilight's soft, embracing gloom,
The shadows stretch, igniting doom.
With silver teeth that glint and shine,
They prowl the edge of dark divine.

Each stealthy step, a lingering tease,
A dance with fate, a silent breeze.
The night unfolds its velvet shroud,
As secrets rise, both fierce and loud.

Beneath the stars, where spirits play,
The shadows weave a bold ballet.
With every twinkle, tales begin,
Of haunted hearts and woven sin.

Yet in this dance, there's beauty found,
A grace that ebbs and flows around.
In silvered teeth, such depth resides,
A truth that even darkness hides.

So tread with care through twilight's spell,
For shadows bind with whispered spell.
In every corner, mysteries sweep,
Where twilight's shadows softly creep.

Moonlit Trails of the Arcane

In moonlit trails, the magic flows,
Where ancient signs and wisdom grows.
Each step reveals a hidden past,
In night's embrace, spells grow vast.

The silver glow, a guiding light,
Illuminates the darkened night.
With whispers soft, the stars conspire,
To weave a fate that won't expire.

Through crooked paths where secrets lie,
The echoes dance, the shadows sigh.
With spells unveiled, and dreams set free,
We walk the trail of mystery.

Among the trees, the spirits stir,
In moonlit glades, the echoes purr.
Each branch a witness to the tale,
In arcane winds, we hear their wail.

So take this journey, brave and bold,
Through moonlit realms where dreams unfold.
In every shadow, magic waits,
To whisper truth through ancient gates.

Secrets of the Verdant Grasp

In the hush of leaves, secrets lie,
Whispers of time, deep and shy.
Roots that twine, a tale unfolds,
Nature's magic in verdant molds.

A flicker of light, a hidden gleam,
Tales of shadows, lost in dream.
Beneath the boughs, where spirits dwell,
Ancient echoes cast their spell.

Branches sway, a dance so bold,
Guardians of stories yet untold.
With every breeze, the past reveals,
The garden's heart, where time congeals.

In emerald shades, young souls run free,
Captured by wonder, forgotten glee.
Each step they take, in laughter bound,
Footprints in hues of mossy ground.

Secrets intricate, woven in green,
In the symphony, silence is seen.
Nature's embrace, a tender find,
In the verdant grasp, all hearts bind.

Moonlight Kisses the Elder Branches

Under a cloak of silver light,
The elder branches reach their height.
Kisses soft from celestial sphere,
In tranquil nights, the dreams appear.

Hushed murmurs float on evening air,
Magic lingers, light as prayer.
In this moment, the world feels right,
Hope ignites as stars take flight.

Vows of whispers, secrets retained,
Under the moon, souls unchained.
An ancient pact, a bond so pure,
In the shadows, hearts endure.

Though time may pass, and seasons change,
The moonlight's glow will rearrange.
Every heart that feels its call,
Answers softly, together we fall.

Elder branches, keepers of lore,
In their embrace, we yearn for more.
Let the night enfold our dreams,
In moonlit dances, love redeems.

Tangles of Fate in the Mystic Glade

In the glade where shadows play,
Fate weaves threads in disarray.
By the brook, a story waits,
Mysterious bonds and whispered fates.

A gentle pull, a woven sigh,
Paths entwined, as moments fly.
Silken strands of joy and pain,
In every twist, a choice remains.

The leaves above, a canopy bright,
Guard secrets held in day and night.
In pulses strong, the glade's embrace,
Echos resonate, time leaves no trace.

Tangles of heartstrings, twirling around,
In this haven, lost ones are found.
Every glance a spark ignites,
In fate's tapestry, our hopes take flight.

Feel the whispers of destiny near,
Within the glade, cast off your fear.
For in these woods, where shadows dance,
Life's tangled fate offers a chance.

Embered Trails Beneath Dark Canopies

Through dark canopies, embers glow,
A path is forged where few may go.
Each flickering light, a beacon bright,
Guides weary hearts through the night.

Crunch of leaves beneath our feet,
The heart of forest, wild and sweet.
Every step, a story told,
In whispered tones, adventures bold.

The canopy sways with secrets vast,
Beneath its embrace, we find our past.
Embers dance in shadows' fold,
Remnants of tales forever old.

Eyes wide open to the magic near,
In the embered trails, we conquer fear.
With each heartbeat, embers spark,
Lighting the way through the dark.

Under starlit skies, dreams ignite,
In the forest's heart, we find our light.
Together we wander, hand in hand,
On embered trails, our spirits stand.

Twisted Paths of the Enigmatic Heart

In shadows deep where whispers play,
A heart beats loud, yet far away.
With every turn, a secret held,
In tangled roots, the truth dispelled.

Through winding trails of fate and chance,
The paths entwined in twilight dance.
A longing gaze, a fleeting spark,
In echoes soft, we chase the dark.

With every sigh the night unfolds,
The stories of the brave and bold.
Yet in the thorns, a beauty lies,
The heart's desire in lowly guise.

Beneath the moon, the silence speaks,
Of ancient woes and mystic peaks.
Adventures call from deep within,
To journeys lost, we dare to spin.

So take my hand, we'll wander far,
Beneath the light of a distant star.
For in this maze of love and art,
We find our truth, the enigmatic heart.

Eldritch Beauty of the Woodland Veil

In dappled light where shadows weave,
The woodland whispers, hearts believe.
A tapestry of emerald hues,
In every leaf, a tale ensues.

The twilight glows with stars anew,
As echoes dance in misty dew.
Through ancient trees, the secrets lie,
Of sylvan dreams that drift and fly.

With every step, the ether sings,
Of magic found in gentle springs.
The fables spun by elder trees,
Their roots entwined with mysteries.

A shiver runs through air so sweet,
Where faerie laughter, soft and fleet.
Reveals the world in vibrant dyes,
In every corner, wonder lies.

The moonlight spills on sylvan ground,
Where whispered lore and love abound.
In eldritch beauty, hearts do sail,
Forever lost in woodland veil.

Lucent Echoes of the Phantom Blossom

In twilight's grasp, the blossoms grow,
With petals bright, a soft, warm glow.
Each ripple dances on the breeze,
A phantom's touch, a lover's tease.

Through moonlit fields where shadows sigh,
The echoes whisper, never shy.
In fragrant dreams, the heart takes flight,
As blossoms beckon through the night.

The tales of love, both lost and found,
In every bloom, their whispers sound.
With every breath, the secrets sing,
Of fleeting time, the joy it brings.

Yet in the dusk, a shadow looms,
The phantom waits in fragrant rooms.
But brave of heart, we chase the light,
Through lucid moments, pure delight.

So let us dance 'neath starry skies,
With lucent echoes as our prize.
For in this night of whispered dreams,
The phantom blossom brightly beams.

Secrets Entwined in the Mossy Bower

In ancient groves, the secrets sleep,
Entwined in moss and shadows deep.
A bower rich with nature's breath,
Holds stories spun from life and death.

The sunbeams break through leafy crowns,
To dance on paths where silence drowns.
In every stone, a voice prevails,
Of travelers lost in winding trails.

With whispers soft, the forest calls,
To hidden realms beyond the walls.
Each breath reveals a ghostly tale,
Of love and loss, a timeless trail.

In clutches green, the secrets nest,
In nature's arms, we find our rest.
This tranquil nook, a refuge rare,
In mossy bower, dreams declare.

So linger here where shadows play,
Let nature's pulse show you the way.
For in the hush of twilight's shroud,
The secrets flicker, soft and loud.

The Gnarled Roots of Magic

In an ancient forest, shadows play,
Where gnarled roots twist in disarray.
Whispers of magic, soft yet clear,
Call to the daring, those who draw near.

A flicker of light in the thickest gloom,
Hints at the wonders that silently bloom.
With every step on the mossy ground,
A heartbeat of secrets, waiting to be found.

Beneath the branches that cradle the sky,
Dreams weave together, daring to fly.
The air is thick with a spellbound sigh,
As the starlit glow begins to pry.

Old stones whisper of lore long past,
Of wizards and witches, their spirits cast.
Through the thickets, the wild songs weave,
Enchanting the hearts that long to believe.

Magic lies deep in the knotted roots,
In every shadow, where wonder shoots.
To those who seek with courage and grace,
A world of enchantment shall they embrace.

Secrets Woven in Silhouettes

In the quiet dusk, shadows blend,
Secrets whisper, hearts mend.
Silhouettes dance upon the walls,
A tapestry of dreams that enthralls.

Beneath the moon's soft, silver light,
Whispers of magic take flight.
The night enfolds the tales of old,
Stories of courage and treasures untold.

Fingers trace the patterns drawn,
In the folds of night, a new dawn.
Every shadow holds a clue,
To mysteries waiting, just for you.

Woven threads of fate collide,
In a dance where secrets hide.
Tickling the air with a gentle tease,
Filling the heart with a tranquil breeze.

In the whispering winds, a promise remains,
That every silence holds no chains.
For those who listen, trust in fate,
Shall find the secrets that resonate.

Echoes of the Hidden Glade

In the heart of woods, a glade concealed,
Where nature's magic is revealed.
Echoes linger in the dew-kissed air,
Of laughter, old tales, memories rare.

Trees stand tall, guardians of the past,
Holding whispers of spells that last.
The softest breeze carries a song,
Of the creatures and magic that belong.

Sunlight seeps through the emerald leaf,
Painting stories of joy and grief.
In the hush of silence, legends arise,
Glimmers of hope beneath the skies.

Footfalls dance on the carpet of shade,
Where secrets and shadows serenely parade.
Listen closely, can you hear their plea?
The echoes of dreams that long to be free.

In the hidden glade, the heart must roam,
Finding solace, a place called home.
For magic and whispers entwine like thread,
In the cradle of dreams, where souls are fed.

Veils of Night and Sorcery

Beneath the veils of midnight's hush,
Where starlit dreams in silence rush.
In whispers dark, the shadows sway,
Carrying the magic of yesterday.

Sorcery brews in the depths of night,
In corners unseen, out of sight.
Each flicker of flame holds a tale,
Of dragons and heroes who dared to fail.

The moon weaves spells with a silver thread,
Binding hearts to the dreams they dread.
With every breath, enchantments blend,
A tapestry of night that seems to mend.

In still, dark woods where the owls sing,
Secrets awaken on whispered wing.
Veiled in silence, the magic flows,
A symphony only the night truly knows.

So wander forth into starlit dreams,
Where magic thrives and softly gleams.
The veils of night hold wonders untold,
A dance of sorcery, brave and bold.

Sigils of the Shadowed Path

Beneath the moon's soft silver glow,
Whispers of secrets ebb and flow,
Footsteps echo on the ground,
Where hidden paths are seldom found.

Shadows dance with ancient grace,
Veils of night, a mystic place,
Markings tell of tales untold,
In silence wrapped, their truths unfold.

The air is thick with magic spun,
A thread of fate, a race begun,
Through darkened woods where fiends do creep,
The heart of night, where visions seep.

Each sigil carved by fate's own hand,
Drawn by dreams, a wizard's brand,
In every flicker, each soft sigh,
Lies a promise to the sky.

So venture forth with steady gaze,
Through shadowed paths, the lost ways blaze,
A journey grand, where spirits dwell,
In secrets kept, they weave their spell.

Treads of the Forest's Grasp

In the heart of the forest dense,
Lies a realm where time's immense,
Ancient trees with wisdom deep,
In their embrace, the secrets sleep.

Footfalls echo on the loam,
In this wild, forgotten home,
Whispers drift on the gentle breeze,
Carried softly through the leaves.

Moss-covered stones sing songs of old,
Tales of bravery, dreams bold,
Paths entwined with emerald light,
Guide the lost through the endless night.

Every step, a story shared,
In the woods, the heart laid bare,
Mysteries twine like ivy's vine,
Each twist and turn, a thread divine.

So stray not far from the forest's plea,
For in its grasp, your soul will be,
Treads of dreams that softly blend,
In nature's arms, find your true end.

Secrets Sheltered by Gnarled Wood

Beneath the branches, twisted, old,
Lies a world with tales untold,
Gnarled wood, a keeper true,
Of whispers soft and skies of blue.

Here the winds of ages sweep,
In every knot, secrets keep,
Time ebbs softly like a stream,
Where every shadow holds a dream.

The dance of leaves, a gentle waltz,
In every rustle, nature's pulse,
Life teems softly, hidden away,
Where magic breathes through night and day.

These secrets spun from silver thread,
In twilight's glow, the stories spread,
The heart of wood, alive and real,
With echoes of the past we feel.

So seek the grove with open mind,
In gnarled wood, the truth you'll find,
For every bark, a tale will stir,
In whispered tones, let spirits blur.

Traces of Celestial Whispers

Above the world, the stars align,
In patterns drawn, the fates entwine,
Whispers drift through twilight's veil,
Soft as the breath of a tender gale.

Celestial lights, they weave and twine,
Guiding hearts with threads divine,
Murmurs of dreams that span the night,
In silence wrapped, they take their flight.

A dance of orbs, a cosmic play,
Drawing wishes near to stay,
Through endless realms where echoes soar,
In whispered tones, hope does restore.

Each glimmer holds a secret bright,
A kiss of dawn, a wish of night,
In every flicker, perhaps a clue,
To paths we chase, the journeys new.

So heed the call of the stars above,
In their embrace, find dreams to love,
For traces left by cosmic hands,
Are stories written in starlit sands.

Whispers Among the Winking Stars

In the hush of silver night,
Where dreams take flight on whispered wings,
Stars in dance, a gentle glow,
Share secrets only starlight brings.

Beneath the kaleidoscopic skies,
Children of wonder gather near,
With laughter bright and hope so bold,
They chase the echoes crystal clear.

Time drifts softly like a feather,
On cosmic winds, the world awakes,
And through the tapestry above,
A spark ignites, the universe shakes.

Each twinkle holds a story slight,
Of courage found and love once lost,
As hearts entwined with fate collide,
They dance beneath the endless frost.

So, listen close and heed the night,
For in the dark, the magic sings,
A symphony of hopes and dreams,
Whispers woven with silver strings.

Veiled Paths of the Bewitched Woods

Where ancient trees in shadows talk,
The paths may twist and turn anew,
With every step, a tale unfolds,
Of secrets known to but a few.

Mossy stones and tangled vines,
Guard hidden doors to realms unknown,
With every breath, enchantments weave,
And spirits linger, softly grown.

Beneath the canopy's embrace,
The air is thick with magic's song,
And those who wander, bold and free,
Will find where they truly belong.

The moonlight dances on the leaves,
A gentle guide through night's embrace,
As whispers echo through the woods,
Inviting all to seek their place.

So follow where the shadows wind,
And trust the heart to lead the way,
In veiled paths of the bewitched woods,
Awaits a new and wondrous day.

Shadows Weave Through Gnarled Roots

In twilight's glow, the shadows play,
Dancing softly through the trees,
With gnarled roots that twist and turn,
Each creak a tale upon the breeze.

Silhouettes of ages past,
Whisper stories steeped in time,
Of dreams once dared, and hopes entwined,
A melody of life's soft chime.

The silent woods, a tapestry,
Of laughter, love, and loss entwined,
As phantom echoes softly breathe,
Into the night, their magic blind.

Through crooked paths and winding trails,
Adventurers brave their hearts do share,
With every footfall, spirits rise,
Among the roots, in dusk-filled air.

So listen well, dear wanderer,
For shadows weave a truth profound,
In gnarled roots, the past shall speak,
With every step upon the ground.

The Enchanted Thorns of Restless Spirits

In gardens where the thorns do grow,
Restless spirits linger near,
With petals soft and whispers low,
They share their tales in twilight's sphere.

A lattice of enchantments spun,
Where roses bloom in shades of dreams,
Amongst the thorns, a magic hums,
And life, it seems, is never what it seems.

They beckon gently to the heart,
With shadows dancing in their wake,
For love is tangled in their roots,
In every choice, a chance to break.

Yet in the thorns, there's beauty rare,
A truth that binds the lost to find,
For every spirit once adrift,
Will seek a path that's intertwined.

So wander here with courage bold,
In enchanted thorns, your fate unspools,
Embrace the dance of somber light,
For restless spirits share their jewels.

The Threshold Beneath the Winking Stars

Beneath the sky of silver light,
A glimmer beckons from the night.
Whispers dance on velvet air,
With secrets spun from dreams laid bare.

The threshold hums with ancient songs,
Where twilight weaves the brave and wrongs.
In shadows deep, the fates entwine,
As time unravels, line by line.

Step forth, where bold hearts dare to trace,
The shimmering paths of wondrous grace.
The stars above, they watch and wait,
For restless souls to tempt their fate.

Each moment holds a chance, a spark,
In realms where journeys leave their mark.
With every breath, let courage grow,
As magic stirs in depths below.

The threshold calls, it's time to see,
The worlds that blend with mystery.
Embrace the night, let wonders unfold,
For tales like these are worth more than gold.

Threads of Fate in the Witchwood Glade

In glades where ferns and shadows greet,
The threads of fate lie soft and sweet.
With every step on mossy ground,
A tapestry of dreams is found.

Moonbeams filter through the leaves,
Where every heart and spirit weaves.
A gentle hum of magic's hand,
Guides the lost to hidden land.

The whispers beckon through the trees,
A dance of fate upon the breeze.
Each thread a story, old yet new,
In witchwood glade where wishes brew.

With every twist and every turn,
A spark ignites, a candle burns.
Embrace the fate your heart desires,
As hopes take flight on starlit fires.

In shadows long and light so rare,
The threads of fate are spun with care.
Follow the path where dreams align,
In witchwood glade, your stars will shine.

Murky Reflections in a Forest Pool

Deep in the woods where echoes live,
A forest pool takes all it can give.
Its surface holds a world untold,
With reflections of the brave and bold.

Beneath the calm, dark secrets lie,
Where tangled dreams and shadows cry.
Each ripple brings a whispered chance,
For those who dare a timid glance.

The water's edge holds stories deep,
Of ancient vows the wild woods keep.
A place where hearts might pause and test,
To find the truth and seek their quest.

The moonlight bathes this tranquil scene,
Reflecting hopes, both shy and keen.
In murky depths, the visions swirl,
Promising magic to the brave and whirled.

So bend your gaze and peer inside,
Where even secrets cannot hide.
For in each droplet, dreams collect,
In the forest pool, let fate connect.

Secrets Eyes Beneath the Branches Lay

In tangled woods where shadows creep,
The secrets hide in silence deep.
With eyes that watch from branches high,
Unseen, they guard the night sky.

A rustle in the underbrush,
Echoes soft, a gentle hush.
For those who linger, those who stray,
Find truths that twist in night and day.

The forest breathes with ancient lore,
As leaves their whispered secrets store.
With every creak and whispered sigh,
The hidden things will rise and fly.

Look closely now, for there you'll find,
A world enchanted, intertwined.
Sights unseen can open doors,
To wondrous lands where magic soars.

So walk with care in twilight's glow,
For secrets eyes are all aglow.
Beneath the branches ever sway,
A realm awaits where spirits play.

A Dance of Leaves in the Witching Wind

In twilight's grasp, the leaves do sway,
Whispering secrets of the fading day.
Each rustle sings a spellbound tune,
As shadows waltz beneath the moon.

The branches bend with timeless grace,
Embracing night in a soft embrace.
While breezes weave through every bough,
A dance of leaves begins right now.

With colors bright, they spin and twirl,
In every nook, their magic swirls.
A haunting call, the wild hearts heed,
In every flutter, a tale is freed.

So let the night with wonder bloom,
As whispers chase away the gloom.
In rustling laughter, spirits rise,
In the dance of leaves, the world complies.

And when the dawn breaks soft and clear,
The echoes linger, drawing near.
With every gust, a promise made,
In every dance, enchantments laid.

Verdant Hues Beneath Starry Veils

Beneath the stars, the leaves unfold,
In shades of green, their stories told.
A tapestry of night entwined,
With dreams and wishes intertwined.

The mossy ground, a whispered spell,
Where secrets hide and fairies dwell.
Emerald dreams in the cool moonlight,
A world transformed, enchanting sight.

The gentle rustle sways the trees,
Their laughter carried on the breeze.
Each verdant hue, a promise bright,
Of magic lingered in the night.

As shadows dance on nature's stage,
The heart of woodland turns the page.
With every breath, the essence flows,
In moonlit glades, the wonder grows.

So find your peace beneath the veil,
Where stars escort the nightingale.
In every leaf, a truth does hide,
In verdant hues, life's dreams abide.

Tales Whispered by Flickering Foliage

In a forest deep where shadows creep,
Flickering leaves their stories keep.
Soft murmurs rise on the evening air,
Tales of enchantment, beyond compare.

Each rustling leaf, a voice that speaks,
Of brave young hearts and daring feats.
In every twist, a legend spun,
Beneath the glow of the setting sun.

Ancient trees with gnarled roots,
Hold close the secrets of past pursuits.
Their branches sway, a beckoning hand,
Inviting wanderers to this land.

A flicker here, a whisper there,
Stories of magic fill the air.
With every crackle underfoot,
A symphony of tales takes root.

So linger here where wonders weave,
In nature's song, embrace believe.
For in each note, a tale ignites,
In flickering foliage, magic lights.

Moonlit Dances Among Feathered Shadows

Under the gaze of the silver moon,
Feathered shadows begin to croon.
With flutters soft, they whirl and dive,
In this midnight dance, they come alive.

As branches sway in gentle grace,
The night unfolds a secret place.
With every beat, the heart takes flight,
In joyous rhythm, pure delight.

The starlit skies, a canvas wide,
As creatures twirl, a wondrous ride.
With whispered calls, the night's alive,
In every flutter, spirits thrive.

Among the shadows, magic thrives,
In every movement, the forest thrives.
As feathers brush against the skin,
In moonlit dances, joy begins.

And when the dawn calls time to part,
The echoes linger in the heart.
For in these nights, the magic flows,
In feathered shadows, wonder glows.

The Murmur of Spirited Ferns

In the glade where shadows play,
Whispers dance among the fronds,
The ferns converse with breezy sway,
Carrying tales of ancient bonds.

Moonlight stitches tiny seams,
Into the fabric of the night,
As every leaf holds secret dreams,
Bathed in soft, ethereal light.

Their voices rise like gentle chimes,
Telling stories of the wise,
In tangled roots, the language rhymes,
Nature's lore beneath the skies.

Each sigh reveals a world of old,
Where faeries learn the art of flight,
And guardians of magic bold,
Caress the fern's green heart with light.

So wander where the ferns are bright,
And heed the murmurs that they weave,
For in each rustle of the night,
Lies a mystery, hard to believe.

Illusions Cast by Cunning Lanterns

In the woods where lanterns glow,
Softly flickering, whispers creep,
They cast their spells on paths below,
Guiding dreamers into sleep.

Each light a trick, a beckoning,
A dance of shadows, sly and bright,
With laughter woven through the ring,
Of fading day and coming night.

Through tangled branches, glimmers play,
Enticing hearts to wander free,
But heed the whispered words they say,
For not all paths lead back to thee.

A fretful sigh, a fleeting shape,
As mystic creatures stretch and yawn,
These lanterns weave a cloak of drape,
That shrouds each truth by break of dawn.

Yet in their glow, small wonders spark,
Where dreams and shadows intertwine,
Seek courage in the hidden dark,
And trust the magic that is thine.

Dreams Cloaked in a Canopy of Night

Under stars that shimmer bright,
A canopy of dreams unfolds,
Veiled in mists of silver light,
Whispers of stories yet untold.

The night draws close, a velvet sigh,
Crickets play a soothing tune,
While visions flutter, drifting by,
Dancing 'neath the watchful moon.

Each breath a wave from worlds afar,
Where wishes sail on gentle streams,
And every heart holds a flickering star,
As magic weaves through sleepy dreams.

With every pulse, the shadows stretch,
Embracing all that seeks to hide,
In this realm, the mind can etch,
The wonders that the heart has spied.

So journey deep where stardust glows,
And let the night your spirit spark,
For in the dark, true magic flows,
Transforming dreams with secrets stark.

The Hedge of Secrets and Cunning Magic

In the heart of a labyrinthine hedge,
Lies a world concealed from light,
Each thorny twist a silent pledge,
Guarding truths from aching sight.

Woven whispers float in the air,
Echoes of laughter lost in time,
As cunning blooms entwine with care,
Casting spells in rhythm and rhyme.

The brambles twist, a barrier bold,
Yet dreams peek through with glimmers bright,
Each secret told, a tale of old,
Hidden within the heart of night.

With every step, the magic stirs,
Inviting those who dare to seek,
A treasure trove of tiny slurs,
In riddles soft and shadows sleek.

So wander deep where few have dared,
And find the spark that lies within,
For in this hedge, the brave are bared,
To uncover where true tales begin.

Wraiths of the Lantern-lit Glen

In shadows deep where whispers dwell,
A lantern flickers—oh, what a spell!
Wraiths dance lightly, draped in night,
Their laughter echoes, a ghostly flight.

Through twisted paths of ancient lore,
Soft secrets buried, dreams to explore.
They beckon gently, the lost to find,
In the glen that shimmers, both cruel and kind.

With lanterns swaying, they weave a tale,
Of love and sorrow, a haunting wail.
Beneath the stars that slowly gleam,
The wraiths will guide you through the dream.

A sighing breeze stirs leaves from rest,
Each whispering wraith, a hidden quest.
In a realm where time cannot confine,
They waltz through ages, both yours and mine.

So linger long where the shadows croon,
In the lantern-lit glen beneath the moon.
For every echo, a wish will sprout,
And your heart's desire shall wander out.

Sylvan Echoes of a Forgotten Spell

In emerald glades where secrets play,
Sylvan echoes call, then fade away.
A tapestry woven of magic's breath,
In whispers soft, it dances with death.

Once upon a time, the trees would sing,
With eldritch tunes of a powerful thing.
The spell forgotten, in hushed repose,
Awaits the seeker among the throes.

A crooning brook, a rustling leaf,
Hides the voice of bygone grief.
Yet here in the heart of the verdant glen,
A spark ignites, and the tale begins.

With every breath, the wood resounds,
Awakening tales long lost, but found.
The spell, it yearns for a hand so bold,
To whisper its charm, let the story unfold.

So tread lightly where the echoes weave,
In twilight's embrace, let the heart believe.
For magic lingers in the wooded vale,
And dreams may stir on a timeless trail.

Ethereal Ribbons in a Twilight Tangle

In twilight's hush where sorrows mend,
Ethereal ribbons twist and blend.
They shimmer softly in dusk's embrace,
A dance of colors, a whispered grace.

With every twist, an untold tale,
Of hearts entwined on a twilight trail.
A flicker of hope in the darkest hour,
The ribbons gleam with a magic power.

Through branches bare, the stars peek through,
Casting light on what is hidden from view.
Each ribbon tells of a wish once made,
In the twilight tangle, dreams cascade.

Lost souls wander, seeking the light,
In the dance of shadows that grace the night.
With courage bright, their fears take flight,
As ribbons of hope take form in sight.

So heed the call of the twilight gleam,
Follow the ribbons into the dream.
For in the tangled paths of the night,
You'll find your heart's desire in the light.

Roots Threaded with Enigmas

Beneath the soil where stories lie,
Roots entwine, reaching for the sky.
Threaded with enigmas, ancient and wise,
They whisper secrets, unseen ties.

In the silent earth, where shadows creep,
Lies a tapestry where memories sleep.
Each twist and turn, a pathway drawn,
To realms of wonder with each new dawn.

Listen closely as the roots impart,
The tales of ages, each beating heart.
A web of life, so intricately spun,
Where beginnings fade, and yet they run.

With every digging, the past reveals,
The laughter buried, the pain it seals.
In the dance of roots, the world takes shape,
An enigma wrapped, a curious drape.

So wander deep where the roots do curl,
Unravel the stories, let your heart twirl.
For in the earth's embrace, you shall find,
The magic of life, forever entwined.

Shadows Dance on Thorns

In twilight's grasp, where shadows loom,
Dance the phantoms, weave the gloom.
Thorns entwined with whispers light,
Guard the secrets hidden tight.

Beneath the stars, the moon's soft glow,
The thorns lie still, watching the show.
Ghostly figures twist and sway,
In a haunting, merry ballet.

With every blink, the night unfolds,
Stories of ancients, forever told.
Winds sing softly through the leaves,
A melody of dreams that weaves.

Each thorn a token, sharp yet fair,
Holds the echoes of the air.
Dance, dear shadows, play your part,
Piercing dark with a tender heart.

So linger long in this mystic trance,
For in the thorns, we find our chance.
A world where secrets ever yearn,
In shadows dance, we brightly burn.

Whispers of the Midnight Grove

In the grove where silence dwells,
Soft whispers weave their secret spells.
Moonbeams dance on leaves of green,
Glimmers bright, like thoughts unseen.

Each rustling branch a tale of yore,
A symphony of nevermore.
Crickets hum a midnight tune,
Underneath the lonesome moon.

Flickering fireflies paint the air,
With fleeting lights, beyond compare.
The shadows pause to listen near,
To every breath both wild and clear.

In every corner, life takes root,
Whether fleeting flame or hidden fruit.
Nature's heartbeat, steady sound,
In the grove, true magic found.

As night unfolds its velvet lace,
We stand still, in a sacred space.
The whispers call, our hearts align,
In the midnight grove, we're divine.

Echoes Through the Hollowed Pines

In the pines, where shadows creep,
Echoes linger, old and deep.
Nature's whispers softly flow,
Brushing hearts with tales we know.

Each wind-blown sigh, a gentle breath,
Speaks of life and speaks of death.
Hollow trunks stand tall and proud,
Guarding secrets 'neath the shroud.

Footsteps echo on the ground,
In this realm, so lost yet found.
Through twisted roots, where light sneaks in,
We chase the dreams that dare to spin.

Birdsong flutters through the leaves,
Telling tales of what believes.
The hollow pines, they hold us close,
In their embrace, we're never lost.

So roam with me, where echoes weave,
Infusing hope in all we believe.
In the pines, where time stands still,
We find our peace, our hearts fulfill.

Glimmers in the Enchanted Thicket

In thickets dense, where magic thrives,
Glimmers dance like brightened lives.
Each flicker tells a tale unknown,
Of dreams forgotten, seeds once sown.

Beneath the leaves of emerald hue,
Lies a world that feels so new.
Misty tendrils greet the dawn,
In enchanted thickets, we move on.

With every step, a secret calls,
As nature's laughter fills the walls.
Rustling whispers weave through air,
Inviting hearts to linger there.

Glimmers shift like stars above,
In this realm of hope and love.
The thicket pulses, alive and bright,
Painting dreams in the dead of night.

So let us wander, hand in hand,
Through veils of green, across the land.
In each glimmer, a story waits,
In the thicket, we find our fates.

Shadows Adrift in the Enchanted Fens

In misty realms where whispers dwell,
The shadows dance, a silent spell.
With footfalls soft on dampened ground,
Lost secrets in the dark are found.

A willow weeps beside the stream,
Beneath the stars, a ghostly gleam.
Each flicker of the firefly's light,
Guides weary souls through the night.

Beneath the moon's enchanting gaze,
The fens come alive in a tender haze.
With every wave of evening's breath,
The air is laced with hints of death.

Yet life persists in shadows' grasp,
A hidden realm within our clasp.
Where every dream and tale is spun,
And promises of dawn begun.

So tread with care through misty mounds,
For ancient magic knows no bounds.
In enchanted fens where shadows drift,
Are stories waiting, a timeless gift.

Gnarled Roots and Wistful Dreams

In forests deep where gnarled roots lie,
Wistful dreams in the branches sigh.
A tapestry of life unfurls,
Beneath the watch of ancient swirls.

The morning dew on emerald blades,
Holds echoes of forgotten glades.
Where creatures small and spirits bright,
Unravel tales in the soft twilight.

With every step, a memory blooms,
As nature sings in wondrous tunes.
The rustling leaves, a friendly cheer,
Awakening hearts, drawing near.

In shadows cast by mighty trees,
Hope dances lightly on the breeze.
And every whisper, every sigh,
Bears tales of dreams that never die.

So wander forth through tangled paths,
With open heart, embrace the laughs.
In gnarled roots and wistful streams,
Find the magic in your dreams.

Shadows of Beauty in the Witching Hour

In the witching hour, shadows play,
Soft and secret, they drift away.
Moonbeams weave through the darkened wood,
Where beauty lingers, misunderstood.

A gentle breeze stirs the night air,
With voices echoing everywhere.
In clandestine glades where starlight blends,
Whispers of love and loss extends.

The crystal pond reflects the sky,
A mirror where lost moments lie.
Each ripple dances, a fleeting kiss,
A moment's grace in the heart of bliss.

Among the trees, the shadows twirl,
In swirling skirts of phantoms' whirl.
Beauty is fleeting, yet ever near,
In whispers of dusk that we long to hear.

So linger awhile, don't rush the night,
Embrace the shadows, hold them tight.
For in the depths of the witching hour,
Lies a beauty wrapped in timeless power.

Enchantments Hidden in the Wild

In thickets dense, where magic hides,
Enchantments bloom by babbling tides.
The wildwood breathes, a secret place,
Where every shadow bears a trace.

In tangled boughs and dappled light,
The forest sings a lullaby bright.
With every petal that falls and sways,
Dreams entwined in the softest ways.

A flicker of wings and a joyful glance,
Reminds us life is a fleeting dance.
In wildflower fields, with colors bold,
Stories of wonder quietly unfold.

The stream meanders, a silken thread,
Through whispers of trees where we dare to tread.
Each droplet holds a tale untold,
Of enchantments whispered in hues of gold.

So venture forth into the wild,
With eyes aglow, like a curious child.
For in the heart of nature's veil,
Lie enchantments waiting to unveil.

Twists of Light Beneath the Boughs

In twilight's glow, the whispers weave,
A dance of shadows, we believe.
With every flicker, secrets sigh,
Beneath the boughs where wishes lie.

The moonlight's embrace, a gentle tease,
The rustling leaves, a haunting breeze.
A tapestry spun from dreams and fear,
In that hush, magic draws near.

Where fireflies blink like stars so small,
And echoes linger, answering the call.
Each twist of light, a path unknown,
Guides us through the twilight's throne.

Beneath the branches, old tales blend,
Of love, of loss, where journeys end.
In every glimmer, a story glows,
Of hearts entwined and fate's delicate throes.

So wander forth, let courage bloom,
In enchanted nights where shadows loom.
For within the light, the truth shall spark,
The magic lives amidst the dark.

Language of Thorns and Shadows

Amongst the thorns where silence grows,
A language speaks that no one knows.
In the tangled depths, dark secrets hide,
Where whispers tremble and fears abide.

With every thorn, a story pricks,
Of ancient hearts and subtle tricks.
The shadows groan, alive with strife,
Echoes of an unseen life.

The midnight air, a velvet shroud,
Enfolds the dreams, both meek and proud.
In this place where light is loath,
The heart learns to dance with both.

Beware the path where shadows creep,
In every thorn, a promise deep.
For hidden truths lie just beyond,
In petals soft, yet fiercely blonde.

So speak the words of darkened day,
Where light retreats and night holds sway.
In the language spun from dread and grace,
Find strength entwined in each embrace.

Mysteries of the Eldritch Grove

In the Eldritch Grove, where shadows dance,
Secrets bloom in a timeless trance.
With twisted limbs and whispers faint,
The wildwood whispers, raw and quaint.

A flicker here, a shimmer there,
With every step, the stories tear.
Ancient echoes blend with the leaves,
As time unravels, the spirit cleaves.

Amongst the roots, old spirits play,
Guardians of night, they hold the sway.
With every gust, the forest sighs,
Bearing witness to ancient ties.

Through misty veils, lost voices call,
In shimmering light where shadows fall.
Each murmur swirls in the twilight's hush,
A call to those who heed the rush.

So wander forth with heart aflame,
In the grove where none are the same.
Embrace the mysteries held so dear,
For in this place, all dreams appear.

Fangs of Midnight's Caress

In the embrace of midnight deep,
Where shadows crawl and secrets creep.
Fangs of desire, silver and sleek,
Unveil the truths we dare not seek.

With every heartbeat, danger sings,
In the stillness, the darkness clings.
The night unfolds in a whispered breath,
A dance with fate, a waltz with death.

Through silken veils of midnight's kiss,
Lurks a longing, an eerie bliss.
With every flicker, the heart takes flight,
Beneath the shroud of starry night.

Where shadows meet with silver light,
And every star reveals a plight.
Fangs of fortune, a perilous play,
In the caress of night, we lose our way.

So tread with caution, dear heart, be wise,
For in the dark, true magic lies.
With every thrill, the senses stir,
In midnight's grasp, our dreams confer.

A Cauldron of Ferns and Moonbeams

In the hush of the glen where shadows play,
Whispers of magic dance in the spray.
Ferns unfurl like secrets to share,
Beneath the soft glow of moonlight's glare.

A cauldron brews with a fragrant sigh,
Stirring enchantments that never die.
Lavender swirls and mint's fresh bite,
Rest in the heart of the starry night.

Bubbles of laughter hang in the air,
As nightingales sing without a care.
Each droplet glimmers with tales untold,
Mysteries woven in silver and gold.

With every drop, the forest dreams,
Adventures unfold in silvery streams.
A potion for friendship, a spell for the bold,
The stories of youth in quiet behold.

And as twilight fades to a gentle sigh,
The cauldron rests beneath the sky.
Ferns sigh softly, a secrets kept,
While moonbeams in reverence quietly stepped.

Dusk's Embrace on Hidden Trails

Dusk wraps the world in a velvet shroud,
Whispers of shadows, a gathering crowd.
Footsteps tread softly on a wandering path,
Nature's soft sighs whisper secrets of wrath.

The trees bend low to the evening's tune,
Beneath the watchful gaze of the moon.
Foxes dart lightly through thickets so deep,
Secrets hidden where wild things creep.

A flicker of light, a firefly's glow,
Guides weary hearts where the wildflowers grow.
The scent of damp earth, the promise of rain,
Calls out to wanderers to be free of pain.

A path veers off where the wild things dwell,
Echoes of laughter in a soothing spell.
Dusk wraps its arms as the stars arise,
Awakening wonder, unveiling the skies.

In every hush lies a silent refrain,
Stories of love, of loss, and of gain.
Dusk fills the heart with a quiet embrace,
As dreams take flight in the shadows' trace.

The Elders' Grove and its Cursed Silence

In the Elders' Grove where shadows loom,
Ancient trees whisper to the silent moon.
Each gnarled branch holds a story old,
Of laughter, of sorrow, and tales retold.

But silence drapes like a shroud in air,
A curse that lingers, heavy with care.
The wind carries murmurs, a ghostly song,
Of a time long lost, where hearts belonged.

Footsteps now echo through the sacred ground,
Where once joyful voices danced all around.
The Elders stand guard, an eternal fight,
Against the encroach of the deepening night.

By the stone altar, the moonlight weeps,
For the secrets the grove so keenly keeps.
A potion brewed from the last twilight,
Holds the key to lift this endless night.

Yet hope like a breeze stirs the air so cold,
As brave souls gather to shatter the mold.
In the silence, a spark ignites the way,
To restore the laughter to the grove's ballet.

Midnight's Chant Amidst the Sycamores

When midnight strikes, the sycamores sway,
In rhythm with whispers of dreams on the way.
A mellow chant threads through the night,
Calling the lost to the heart of the light.

Branches like arms embrace the dark,
Crickets joining in with their sharp, bright spark.
As shadows entwine, the world feels alive,
In this soft cradle, the lost can thrive.

Moonbeams flicker like jewels on the stream,
Reflecting the secrets, the hopes, and the dream.
From the heart of the grove, an echo flows,
As nature dances, the darkness bestows.

In this sacred space where silence hums,
The spirit of midnight gently comes.
With every note, the fabric weaves tight,
Binding the stars to the peace of the night.

And as dawn creeps in with a gold-hued kiss,
The song of the sycamores fades into bliss.
A promise that echoes with every breath,
In the heart of the night, life conquers death.

Where the Nightingale Weaves

In the quiet glade where moonlight sings,
The nightingale weaves her silver threads.
With whispers soft as the gentle breeze,
She gathers dreams from feathered beds.

Underneath the boughs, shadows dance,
As starlit hopes begin to twine.
Each note a spell, a fleeting chance,
To weave the dreams of night divine.

Her melodies float on the cool night air,
Carrying wishes to worlds unseen.
In the gilded hush, no sound to spare,
The nightingale reigns, a queen serene.

Among the flowers that brave the dark,
She writes her tales on leaves so fair.
Moments captured, each a spark,
Of restless hearts that linger there.

So listen close, when the stars align,
To the song that weaves the endless night.
For in her notes, the fates entwine,
And magic dances in the light.

Sylvan Threads of Ancient Lore

Beneath the ancient trees, wisdom wakes,
Tangled roots that cradle time's embrace.
In whispers low, the forest speaks,
Of secrets held in a verdant place.

Through canopies draped in emerald hue,
The air is thick with stories long gone.
Sylvan threads of an olden queue,
Binding the past in a fragrant dawn.

Each rustling leaf, a page turned slow,
Unveiling tales of joy and strife.
In the heart of the woods, a gentle glow,
Illuminates the magic of life.

The brook sings softly as it flows,
A melody of ages, hushed and pure.
With every ripple, the past bestows,
A timeless bond that shall endure.

So wander deeper, where shadows merge,
And let the whispers guide your way.
In sylvan threads, let your spirit surge,
For here, the ancients still hold sway.

Thorns Crowned in Twilight

When twilight's veil cloaks the fading light,
The thorns stand proud in their shadowed grace.
With petals soft, a heart's true plight,
They guard the beauty, a fleeting trace.

In tangled thickets where secrets lie,
The roses bloom, yet hold a sting.
In their embrace, the truths we spy,
Of love and loss, and what they bring.

Beneath the stars, the thorns entwine,
A fortress fierce, yet softly sweet.
And in their grasp, a heart's design,
To feel the joy, to bear the heat.

In every cut, a lesson learned,
Of beauty found in shadows cast.
Though pain may come, the heart has yearned,
For love that's deep, that holds us fast.

So tread with care, where thorns may reign,
For in their midst, a treasure glows.
In twilight's hush, through joy and pain,
The crown of thorns, the heart, bestows.

Enigmas Linger in the Forest's Breath

In the depth of woods where echoes dwell,
The air is thick with whispers low.
Enigmas linger, a mystic spell,
In every corner where shadows grow.

Moonlight weaves through branches bare,
Casting shapes that flit and glide.
A dance of secrets, silent and rare,
Where ancient spirits often bide.

Each rustling leaf keeps tales untold,
Of wanderers lost and dreams they chased.
In the forest's breath, the night unfolds,
A riddle framed in nature's grace.

The words of lore flutter like a moth,
Intrigued by flames that draw them near.
So listen well, but tread with troth,
For truths may come with quiet fear.

In whispered sighs, the forest speaks,
Of journeys past and futures bright.
Embrace the enigmas, let your heart seek,
The magic hidden in the night.

The Forest's Breath

In the hush of twilight's glow,
Leaves whisper secrets, soft and low.
Each breeze carries tales unknown,
In the forest's heart, magic is sown.

Mossy carpets beneath our feet,
A symphony of dusk, bittersweet.
Ancient trees with stories to share,
The forest breathes, a watchful stare.

Crickets sing as shadows creep,
In their songs, the night is deep.
Stars flicker, a celestial dance,
In the stillness, we take a chance.

Flickering lights of fireflies bright,
Guide our hearts through the velvety night.
Every rustle, a whispered call,
In this sanctuary, we find it all.

So listen close, let spirits weave,
In the forest's breath, we believe.
Magic lives in the unseen space,
Where nature and souls intertwine in grace.

Ghostly Lullabies

Through the mist, where shadows play,
Ghostly lullabies softly sway.
Under the moon's silver embrace,
Restless spirits find their place.

Echoes linger in the night air,
Haunted whispers, a gentle care.
In the silence, they softly croon,
Stories bathed in the light of the moon.

Dreamers walk on paths of mist,
Guided by a translucent twist.
Each note carries a tale of old,
In ghostly lullabies, dreams unfold.

Shadows dance in a tender sway,
Lost in the song of yesterday.
Every breeze a tender sigh,
As the night drapes the world awry.

So close your eyes, let memories flee,
In the arms of the night, be free.
For in this hush, where spirits bide,
Ghostly lullabies gently guide.

Echoes of the Forgotten Grove

In a grove where time stands still,
Echoes linger on every hill.
Whispers of those who came before,
In the stillness, their shadows soar.

Worn path leads to ancient trees,
Carved by hands that felt the breeze.
Each sigh, a story, lost yet near,
In the echoes, we hold them dear.

Dreams entwined in woven roots,
Nature sings in her leafy suits.
Sunlight dapples the forest floor,
A rich tapestry of tales galore.

In the silence, a gentle song,
Of souls who wandered, where they belong.
Hands raised high to the azure sky,
In their murmur, we remember why.

So linger long in the shaded light,
Find the echoes that feel just right.
For in the grove, where whispers flow,
The past resides, forever aglow.

Whispers of Bewildered Wanderers

Among the trees where wanderers roam,
Echoing dreams lead us back home.
Feet on paths of fern and vine,
In nature's chaos, stars align.

Whispers float through the cool night air,
Stories lost, yet hearts laid bare.
Laughter dances on the night's breath,
In shadows, we find a glimpse of depth.

Stars are watchful, their glow we trace,
With bewildered steps, we find our place.
Each rustling leaf a siren's call,
We wander through the midnight's sprawl.

A moonbeam guides our halting pace,
Through tangled woods, we wander through space.
In every sigh, a tale unfolds,
Of hearts entwined, brave and bold.

So take a breath, let magic weave,
In whispers, our spirits believe.
For every wanderer, lost yet free,
Finds the path that leads to dreams.

Tales Woven in the Moonlit Thicket

In the thicket where shadows dwell,
Moonlit tales swirl like a spell.
Branch and blossom, life in bloom,
Lay secrets danced in the night's loom.

Crickets chirp a rhythmic tune,
As fireflies flicker beneath the moon.
Each whispering leaf, a story told,
In the embrace of night, so bold.

Among the fog, the light entwines,
Woven stories in tangled vines.
Every glimmer, a spark of light,
In the thicket, dreams take flight.

With shadows cast and spirits near,
Hold close the truth, hold close the fear.
For in these tales, both dark and bright,
We find our courage, our endless flight.

So in the moonlit thicket, stay,
Let the night carries worries away.
For here, woven with silken thread,
Are the stories of the living and the dead.

www.ingramcontent.com/pod-product-compliance
Ingram Content Group UK Ltd.
Pitfield, Milton Keynes, MK11 3LW, UK
UKHW021448280125
4335UKWH00035B/440

9 781805 638834